D0530599

Time-saving books that teach specific skills to busy people, focusing on what really matters; the things that make a difference – the *essentials*. Other books in the series include:

Pass Your Practical Driving Test

Writing Good Reports

Feeling Good For No Good Reason

Responding to Stress

Succeeding at Interviews

Solving Problems

Writing Successful Essays

Getting Started on the Internet

Boost Your Word Power

Making the Best Man's Speech

Making Great Presentations

Making the Most of Your Time

For full details please send for a free copy of the latest catalogue. See back cover for address.

The things you need to know to

Make Exams Easy

Mike Evans

ESSENTIALS

First published in 2001 by
How To Books Ltd, 3 Newtec Place,
Magdalen Road, Oxford OX4 1RE, United Kingdom
Tel: (01865) 793806   Fax: (01865) 248780
email: info@howtobooks.co.uk
www.howtobooks.co.uk

British Library Cataloguing in Publication Data.
A catalogue record for this book is available from
the British Library.

Edited by Diana Brueton
Cover design by Shireen Nathoo Design
Produced for How To Books by Deer Park Productions
Typeset by Anneset, Weston-super-Mare, Somerset
Printed and bound in Great Britain by The Baskerville Press Ltd.

NOTE: The material contained in this book is set out in good faith for
general guidance and no liability can be accepted for loss or expense
incurred as a result of relying in particular circumstances on
statements made in the book. Laws and regulations are complex and
liable to change, and readers should check the current position with
the relevant authorities before making personal arrangements.

ESSENTIALS *is an imprint of*
How To Books

Contents

Preface

Exams tend to promote feelings of fear, dread and worry in many people. Many myths surround the whole topic, eg that exams are designed to catch you out, or that luck plays a key part in your chances of success. Many think that success is only for:

- the very clever
- the extremely hard working
- those with a photographic memory, etc.

These feelings all conspire to reduce confidence and turn otherwise capable individuals into nervous wrecks at exam time. But it needn't be like this and *you can actually make exams easy*.

This book offers some simple tools, insights and approaches which will really make the difference in exam performance. It isn't just hard work or intelligence that gets you through. In fact many hard working, intelligent people fail through poor exam technique. At least 50 per cent of your chances are down to:

- The way you choose to view exams.
- How you approach your course of study with the exam in mind.
- Simple but effective techniques to use in the exam itself.

These techniques are easy to learn and proven beyond doubt. They also have the added advantage of giving your confidence a welcome boost so that you arrive in the exam room ready and able to succeed.

Mike Evans

1 So What's the Big Deal?

Exam success isn't only for the clever and hard working. Success comes as much, if not more, from your attitude to exams, the way you approach the course of study and some simple techniques to use on the day itself.

4

things that
really matter

1   **GETTING A SENSIBLE PERSPECTIVE**

2   **UNDERSTANDING WHAT CAN GO WRONG**

3   **MANAGING STRESS**

4   **ADOPTING A POSITIVE APPROACH AND TAKING CONTROL**

A universal culture of fear, worry and stress has developed around exams. But it needn't be like this for you. This book dispels the common myths and shows you how to adopt a positive and confident approach. Some simple insights, tools and approaches are provided which are rarely taught in schools and colleges, but which can really make the difference between success and failure. In fact they are likely to account for 50 per cent of your chances of success.

Those who apply the techniques illustrated in this book will gain an immediate advantage over the not-so-enlightened. This advantage comes from changing your approach throughout the course of study and on the day of the exam itself; and through *building confidence* - the all-too-often missing ingredient which can reduce intelligent, capable people to nervous wrecks at exam time.

IS THIS YOU?

● I can cope with most things in life but exams really worry me. ● One of the things I hate about exams is the way they always try to catch you out.
● Exams seem to be more a test of memory and how you can cope with stress than whether you understand the subject itself. ● The stress created by having to do exams can be very harmful. ● You can only do well if you think and write quickly.

① GETTING A SENSIBLE PERSPECTIVE

Let's dispel a few myths straight away.

1   Exams are not designed to catch you out. They test your understanding in a constructive way. Questions are designed to let you demonstrate your abilities rather than expose weaknesses. They are framed in a way that minimises or eliminates any misunderstanding about what is required. It has to be like this to ensure that the marking process is fair.

What is usually misinterpreted as too exacting is nothing more than an honest attempt at clarity.

2   Examiners are not beasts. Think about it. They are usually from the teaching profession so they understand and sympathise with students. For internally set exams they are often your own tutors and your failure could reflect badly on them. I'm certainly not suggesting that they would award a pass where it isn't justified, but they're on your side and have no interest at all in catching you out unfairly.

Examiners actually want you to pass. They like awarding marks!

3   Examiners do not want to catch you out. But they expect you to do what is asked.

The only 'catching out' that goes on is when candidates catch themselves out through not reading the question properly.

4   You can make it easy for examiners to award marks. If you read the requirements carefully and structure your answers accordingly then there are some great benefits to be had. The examiner has a pre-determined marking scheme geared to the exact requirements of the question.

By answering what is required you make it easy for the examiner to allocate marks.

5   Exams are not usually designed to test your memory. They test your understanding and ability to apply concepts. This requires you to remember a degree of detail but that's not what you are being tested on.

Don't worry about how good your memory is. It will be good enough if you have organised your notes and course material and undertaken sufficient revision.

6   Exams are not tests of writing and thinking speed. Sure there's no time for a leisurely coffee break and you need to work fairly quickly, but this actually helps bring out the best in you.

There is a limit to what you can do in 45 minutes so no one expects an exam answer to be a literary work of art.

The commonly *perceived* problem of insufficient time is usually because candidates:

- Manage their time badly.

- Try to write all they know about something (that is, treat it as a memory test – which it isn't) rather than select the parts which are relevant to the question.

- Fail to organise their answers effectively.

The exam is designed to be capable of completion in the allotted time.

② UNDERSTANDING WHAT CAN GO WRONG

If you don't do much work, and you do little or no revision, then you'll probably fail and you deserve to. But even capable, hard working students can fail for any of a number of reasons including:

- The negative effects of stress and exam nerves.

- Relying solely on the tutor to teach them everything.

- Poorly planned and ineffective revision.

- Poor note-keeping which makes revision difficult.

- Poor essay technique.

- Failure to manage time effectively during the exam.

- Failure to read questions properly.

- Failure to plan answers carefully.

The good news is that all these things can be avoided easily and I'll show you how later. For now all you need is a general awareness of the sort of things that can and regularly do go wrong. A combination of:

- the right mental attitude

- well organised notes

- well planned revision

- proper exam technique

. . . is *at least* as important as the course content itself. Accept this and you're well on the way to making this book really work for you.

I have known cases where students didn't do enough work but achieved a pass through using these techniques. In fact this has happened to me on more than one occasion. I'm certainly not suggesting that you try to get by with as little work as possible – that's far too risky – but I am emphasising the importance of what you are about to learn.

The techniques in this book are proven beyond doubt and are easy to understand and apply. They have been used successfully by myself, my students, colleagues, friends and my own children.

The approach is *relevant to almost any type of exam* whether professional or academic, Masters level or GCSE, essay or multiple choice.

 MANAGING STRESS

Exams can cause a lot of stress. This book is designed to minimise, or hopefully eliminate, the negative effects by removing some of the common myths about exams and helping you take control of the process yourself. But there's more to it than that. The pressure of exams can actually create some positive forces. Many people will tell you that they perform better under pressure. More often than not, crises actually bring out the best in people. A certain amount of anxiety will help you to do well.

The trick is to harness the positive aspects of stress and minimise the negative effects.

How you achieve this will depend very much on the type of individual you are. What works for one person will not necessarily work for all. There is a wealth of literature on stress management covering such things as:

- exercise and diet

- relaxation techniques

- natural therapies

- positive thinking etc.

If you haven't already done so, you may find it useful to try some of these.

View stress as a two-edged sword as far as exams are concerned. Look for the positive side. See exams as *an opportunity to do well and achieve more than you might otherwise.* By improving your understanding of what examiners require you can build your confidence and get rid of some of the misconceptions and myths.

Many argue that the exam system puts terrible stress on young people and this sometimes has tragic consequences. This stress is more often than not founded on irrationality and those who experience extreme symptoms should seek medical help immediately. This book can help anyone feel much better about exams. Life puts many stresses on the young and learning to cope with exams can help them in later life. Many actually learn to thrive on stress through seeing the various challenges as opportunities to do well.

④ ADOPTING A POSITIVE APPROACH AND TAKING CONTROL

The very mention of the word exams usually creates negative thoughts. Let's start to get rid of these right now. We've already established that:

- Exams are not designed to catch you out.

- They provide an opportunity for you to demonstrate your abilities.

- Examiners like giving marks to people who do what is asked of them.

- Exams can be completed in the allotted time.

- Everyone's memory is sufficient.

Add to this the fact that you have probably chosen to undertake the course and you almost certainly wouldn't be doing it if you haven't got what it takes. Think also about the positive outcomes when you succeed.

Obviously you want to pass, the examiners want you to pass, your tutors want you to pass and I'm sure your family and friends want you to pass. That's a lot of positive vibes before you even start. In fact there appears to be a grand conspiracy in your favour so don't let a few negative, irrational thoughts spoil it.

The various sources of help available, which few take advantage of, will be highlighted in this book. Students who cocoon themselves in an isolated state of helplessness are making things unnecessarily difficult. There's a lot of help around, all you have to do is make a little effort to secure it.

Don't even begin to think that luck plays a major part. There will always be some elements of the course that you feel more comfortable with than others, and you will no doubt feel better if questions come up on those. You could say that luck features in such cases but overall this isn't a make-or-break factor in exam success. You can take control of the whole process right from the start, through your revision and by how you approach the exam itself. We'll talk also about essay technique and exam technique generally.

By the time you've read this book you will be feeling confident in your approach, leaving any thoughts of luck to your chances in the National Lottery.

MAKING WHAT MATTERS WORK FOR YOU

✓ Remember that no one is trying to catch you out. Careful reading of a carefully framed question provides the opportunity for you to do well.

✓ The common causes of failure are easy to avoid. Make sure you understand them.

✓ Recognise the positive aspects of stress and find out how to minimise the negative effects.

✓ Recognise and take advantage of the fact that everyone, *including the examiner,* wants you to pass.

2 Start Planning for Success Now

A well planned campaign makes life easier, builds confidence and virtually guarantees success

things that really matter

1 **FAILING TO PLAN IS PLANNING TO FAIL**

2 **MAINTAINING A POSITIVE OUTLOOK**

3 **STARTING TO THINK ABOUT THE EXAMS – NOW**

4 **FINDING HELP AND INFORMATION**

Finding time to study and prepare for exams is a challenge for most students. Parents with full-time jobs studying by distance learning will experience many demands on their time. Even full-time students will find that they have too much to do. Part-time jobs, holidays and a social life all conspire to fill their time. As deadlines approach, pressure and anxiety mount and it can all seem to get a bit much.

It may appear at first that I'm adding to the problem by suggesting that you do more towards your exams than you might otherwise have done. But please don't throw the book away just yet. Overall, you won't be any worse off timewise. The extra effort from the outset will reduce last minute cramming. More importantly, you'll feel much more positive about the whole situation, and do better as a result. It's linked with the idea of taking control to build confidence and guarantee success.

IS THIS YOU?

● I have far too many calls on my time to do as well as I'd like to in the exams. I just lurch from crisis to crisis, deadline to deadline and I can't seem to do anything properly. ● I expect my teacher/tutor to prepare me properly for the exam by covering the right things and setting suitable assignments and mock exams. ● No one has the time to do justice to the mock exams and we'll all do better when the real thing comes around. ● I'll start thinking about the exams as we approach the end of the course. I'm certainly not going to worry about them yet, I'll only get depressed if I do.

1 FAILING TO PLAN IS PLANNING TO FAIL

Life would be very boring if we planned everything and only did the things we scheduled exactly in line with our intentions. Spontaneity and surprise can add much-needed excitement to our everyday existence. Unfortunately, where exams are concerned it really is vital that you *plan properly*. Spontaneity and surprise become panic and stress if you don't and you should avoid these at all costs. You must:

● Plan for the exam itself.

● Plan to fit your studying and revision into your lifestyle generally.

Start thinking about all the things that you'll need to do for the exam. In particular:

● Getting hold of past exam papers and practising questions under exam conditions.

● Completing coursework assignments.

● Setting aside time for revision.

You must revise seriously for mock exams (we'll talk more about **revision** in Chapter 3). This will actually make your final revision much easier and quicker to complete.

Mock exams are a golden opportunity for rehearsing the real thing.

When you've gathered all this information you will need to begin drafting an **outline plan** covering the period from now until the exam. Highlight deadlines for coursework assignments as well as dates for the mock exams and the real ones. Plan the revision periods for both. These dates are immovable so you must plan other commitments around them. You can then allocate provisionally periods for the more discretionary tasks, eg practising exam questions.

All of this now needs looking at alongside your other commitments in life such as:

- holidays

- Christmas, birthdays and anniversaries

- busy periods relating to any full or part-time jobs

- important dates for leisure pursuits.

Your outline plan should now include these. *You may have to make a few decisions on priorities.* For example, a weekend away with the tennis club may not be a good idea just before an exam. Similarly, repainting the garden fence can wait a while whereas revision can't.

Exams won't be with you all your life so a few sacrifices now will prove worthwhile in the longer term.

Don't over-commit yourself and be prepared to say 'No' if asked to take on extra commitments. Don't make life unnecessarily difficult for yourself.

Friends, family and employers are likely to be sympathetic if you explain that you have some critical dates relating to your studies which conflict with other activities.

Get a clear idea of your commitments for the next nine months or so, thereby highlighting where time constraints could cause difficulties. You can then establish priorities and schedule your time to avoid having to complete an impossible amount in a short time. In this way you will minimise stress and avoid not having time to do any of the conflicting things well.

You may wish to supplement this plan with more detailed plans covering the next month or even the coming week. The degree of detailed planning required depends very much on what will work for you.

Plan your commitments and take control of your time so you don't suddenly get caught out.

Finally, in planning your studies you may find it useful to consider where, when and how you will study. For example:

- How best to maintain your notes and revision aids, eg revision cards, highlight pens, loose leaf systems, etc.

- The times of day which suit you best for studying.

- Whether you have suitable facilities at home for studying and how much must be done at college/school because you need access to study aids, the Internet, audio visual facilities, scientific equipment, research data, etc.

- Negotiating uninterrupted study time with your partner, family, room mates, etc.

- Whether you will use a computer for note-keeping (and if so, back up and store files securely)

② MAINTAINING A POSITIVE OUTLOOK

You have every right to be optimistic. You saw why in Chapter 1 and as you progress through each chapter you will learn things to reinforce this. *Taking responsibility for your own success* is a key component here. Relying solely on your tutor to equip you with everything you need for success is dangerous. How often have you heard candidates leaving an exam room saying 'we didn't cover half the stuff that came up.'

The day of the exam itself is not the time to find out that you haven't covered the syllabus, and being able to blame a tutor is absolutely no consolation.

Tutors are no different from members of any other profession. They're not infallible and there are good ones and bad ones. Time constraints often mean that they exclude certain elements and this may be appropriate if the exams provide sufficient choice for this not to be a problem. But this may be a risky strategy – risky for you, that is, not the tutor!

Rather than entrust your future completely to them there are things you can do to avoid getting caught out:

- Get hold of a copy of the syllabus.

- Ask the tutor if they expect to cover everything.

- Monitor your progress throughout the course to see whether you're covering everything.

- If not, try to establish the level of risk.

- Study the missing elements

Other important things you should do to maximise your chances are explained below. These are unlikely to be promoted by your tutors. Nowadays education and personal development operates much more on a basis of individuals taking responsibility for their own learning.

The best person to look after your interests is you.

STARTING TO THINK ABOUT THE EXAMS – NOW

It's no good thinking about the course itself as a separate element from the exams. From the outset of the course you must *continually think about the final exams*. This doesn't mean that you should give yourself a regular shot of anxiety about the dreaded final test to spur yourself on, but that you consider how what you have studied today might fit into an exam question. For example, today's economics student would recognise the topicality of the single European currency and pay particular attention to the various viewpoints being promoted in the media.

Course topics which appear to be open to differing viewpoints are good subjects for questions which ask you to 'Discuss the advantages and disadvantages of . . .' Make sure you:

- Identify and explore these as you go along.

- Ask your tutors to highlight the main points.

- Make brief notes for later revision and discuss them with fellow students. Ideas and arguments are likely to earn you the marks in an exam, and you'll get many more talking to others than thinking about it alone.

You are unlikely to be asked simply to 'Write all you know about . . .' Remember the exam is not a memory test.

Don't slavishly absorb the course content without thinking how it might present itself in an exam question. The best time to think about it is as you study each element.

Get hold of **past exam papers** and see what type of questions come up. Familiarise yourself with the **format** of the exam paper and look for patterns. Consider how your current studies may translate into **typical questions**.

④ **FINDING HELP AND INFORMATION**

You need to find out all you can about the exam you're going to take. Your tutor is obviously a useful source of information but there are others.

- Talk to people who have already passed the exam (they'll be quite flattered). Ask if there are any particular points to look out for. You never know what they might have found out themselves. You may even find that some of them know an examiner for the subject who will have given them some valuable pointers.

- Get hold of past exam papers and model answers, and pay particular attention to *how* the questions have been answered. We'll be talking much more about this later.

- Practise answering questions under exam conditions. You'll often find that your tutors will issue an open offer to mark any practice questions which students care to attempt. It's also fairly common for students not to bother unless the essay is a set requirement of the course. Talk about looking a gift horse in the mouth!

One of the most valuable things you can do in preparing for an exam is to practise past questions and then get some constructive feedback from someone who knows the subject. Practising past questions helps hone your essay technique as well as preparing you for planning and answering questions in a limited time. The famous golfer Arnold Palmer once said 'The more I practise, the luckier I seem to get'.

- Get hold of Examiners' Reports for exams. Virtually every one will comment on evidence of students *not managing their time effectively and not addressing the precise requirements of the question* (we'll talk about this later). But you may find that they'll also include comments on technical issues relevant to that particular subject.

- Where course materials seem a little sketchy or you need some more information, don't forget that libraries and the Internet are invaluable sources.

- Discuss the course generally, or each lecture specifically, with your course colleagues and *ascertain the key points* as well as sorting out any queries you may have. Between you, there probably isn't any technical issue that you can't resolve. Nurture these relationships and support each other.

Finally, if you find that things start to worry you, that you are struggling to keep up or even if issues in your private life are affecting your studies – *get some help.* Not necessarily serious therapy, but there are fairly straightforward, readily available sources of support. Talk to your course colleagues, most of whom will probably experience similar anxieties at some stage. You'd be amazed how a sympathetic ear can often make you feel so much better and help you regain a sense of perspective. You may wish to talk to your tutor who will almost certainly be sympathetic and who, in all probability, will be able to offer some useful, practical help. Talk to your family, your friends, your partner and your employer all of whom are likely to provide at least moral support which may be all that's needed.

MAKING WHAT MATTERS WORK FOR YOU

✓ Plan the key requirements, commitments and milestones for the period from now until the exam. Deal with any hot spots.

✓ Stay positive and remember that you're the best person to look after your interests.

✓ Consider everything you learn in the context of a possible exam question.

✓ Identify and use all the sources of help available to you.

3 Dealing with Revision

*Revision isn't just about setting aside time
for last minute cramming. There are easier,
more enjoyable and more effective ways.*

4 things that
really matter

1   UNDERSTANDING ACTIVE REVISION

2   STARTING REVISION WHEN THE COURSE BEGINS

3   ORGANISING NOTES AND OTHER COURSE MATERIALS

4   PLANNING YOUR FINAL REVISION

Having dispelled some myths about exams I'm now going to dispel a few about revision. Most students view revision as something that has to be left until the end of the course and which involves a long, boring slog through the course materials with the sole aim of memorising the content. Fortunately, that's not the best way to ensure success and it needn't be that boring or painful. *Your revision should start at the beginning of the course* to minimise the effort needed at the end.

Some try to minimise the pain by looking for trends in past exam papers, guessing what is likely to come up, then revising only those topics. That's far too risky if you're serious about success. There's a much better way. It's an approach that will provide a much better focus on what you must do to be successful as well as spreading the workload and making the whole thing less boring.

IS THIS YOU?

● I don't mind all the coursework but revision really kills me. It's just a long, boring read through my notes in the hope that I can memorise enough to impress the examiner. ● I have to leave revision until the last minute because if I start too early I'll forget everything.

● Revision is all the more difficult because of the sheer volume of notes, press cuttings and magazine articles that I accumulate throughout the course and which must be sorted out before I can begin memorising everything. ● I feel very isolated when I'm cramming and if I suddenly find I don't understand something it may be too late to get some help.

UNDERSTANDING ACTIVE REVISION

In Chapter 1 we saw that exams are not a test of memory but rather a test of **understanding**. So it follows that your whole approach to revision should be geared towards demonstrating your understanding of the course. You do need to remember the main points in order to apply this understanding, but the prime focus should not be on memorising. Some things that you are required to remember are best left to the last minute, eg scientific or mathematical formulae, but these are not what revision is all about.

Approach your revision in a way that is geared to understanding and constructive criticism of course topics. This will help you remember everything you need.

You saw also in Chapter 1 that you will not be required to 'Write all you know about . . .' a subject. The danger in viewing revision as a task of memorising is that you will prepare yourself simply to regurgitate facts. A prime objective of this book is to prevent you from doing that.

Right from the start think of revision as **preparation** to provide clear, focused answers to exactly what the examiner asks. This involves being able to understand the various viewpoints or aspects of a particular topic so that you can develop reasoned responses to questions aimed at testing your understanding. You need to develop this approach, something I call **Active Revision,** so that it becomes second nature throughout the course. In this way you will reduce the time needed for final revision as well as being much better equipped to provide suitable answers.

Active Revision involves looking for and understanding the key points and arguments associated with each topic as you progress through the course, and thinking how these may manifest themselves in exam questions.

Contrast this with **Passive Revision** which is the process of memorising the facts just before the exam, with the aim of simply regurgitating facts.

There's even more to it than that. Active Revision also involves practising past and potential exam questions so that you can express this *newly-found level of understanding* in a coherent and concise manner in the time available. This should include some practice of questions under exam conditions, but you don't have to go to these lengths for every question you look at. For most you need only compile an **essay plan** of the main points to clarify your thoughts (we'll be talking about essay plans later).

 STARTING REVISION WHEN THE COURSE BEGINS

You may question the value of starting to revise at the beginning of the course, when you've learned very little and feel you're likely to forget it anyway. However, you need to change your traditional perception of the word 'revision'. I'm talking about a different approach, which involves *thinking about everything in a wider sense,* not simply absorbing facts – thinking about everything in the context of a *potential* exam question. This requires little effort at the time but will make your final revision much easier. It also means that you will do much better in the exams.

Do not view the course work and revision as completely separate processes. Revision is part of the learning process.

It is a common mistake for students to see the course as simply a process of taking in facts, and revision as a separate, final, activity where these facts are memorised to be replayed to the examiner. What you must now recognise is that *some revision activities need to be carried out as an integral part of the course.*

You saw above that Active Revision means looking for and understanding the **key points** and **arguments** associated with each topic *as you progress through the course,* and thinking how these may manifest themselves into exam questions. It needs to become second nature, so begin practising this as soon as you start the course. It doesn't require much extra effort, whereas the payoff at exam time will be immense.

So how do you do it? Actually it's very easy and will also make the course more interesting for you.

- For each lecture, class or course unit (for distance learning), identify the **important components**. You're likely to have noted these down in class but the strange thing is that you don't actually learn very much simply by taking notes.

● Review your notes shortly afterwards.

In doing so you will consolidate your learning and ease your final revision by committing the details more firmly to your long-term memory. This is because the key points will have been highlighted already and you will have quickly carried out a first review of the material.

Each time you review something, it's easier to recall later.

● Get hold of past exam papers early on so that you can see, as you work through the course, what sort of questions have been asked on each topic in the past.

● Periodically answer a past question *under exam conditions*. This is best done immediately after you've studied a particular topic to avoid the need for extensive revision. If you do one question every few weeks you'll find it much easier to cope with the exam.

● For each topic ask yourself 'what might an exam question on this look like?' Some topics lend themselves more readily than others to discussion, differing views or advantages/disadvantages. So look out for these and, *after each class*, make some brief notes on the likely questions and how you would answer them.

● Share your thoughts on both the key points and potential questions with course colleagues. This is best done in a group of three or four students. Coffee breaks etc can be a useful time to do this, or you may wish to formalise the arrangements with a regular get-together.

Many students these days are finding that setting up **self-help groups** really increases their understanding of the course, with pleasing results at exam time. A brief review and chat amongst yourselves in a small group will:

- Achieve a common understanding of the key points.

- Let you share ideas on likely exam questions.

- Give those who didn't understand any particular points a chance to get clarification from the others.

But there's also another great advantage. Constructive discussions like this can help *build confidence* for everyone taking part. However, not everyone is comfortable with group work and the less confident must not allow themselves to feel intimidated by the cleverer course participants, but it's very important that you share your thoughts with at least one other student. So choose carefully exactly who you wish to work with. *The aim must be mutual support and benefit for all participants.* This means that:

- Everyone should prepare in advance for the session.

- It's important for all those involved to contribute.

- You should not allow a situation to develop where these sessions become a vehicle for the more gifted to show off or for the more vociferous to hog the proceedings.

Whilst we're talking about what exam questions for each topic might look like, it's worth thinking about the fairly common practice of *guessing which topics are likely to come up* in your exam. Students do this to minimise the amount of final revision they have to do, but it is always a risky strategy. It's less risky in some cases, where the structure of the exam offers a high degree of choice. But even then it's often choice *within* a whole part of the syllabus, meaning that you have to cover all topics.

If you're serious about success don't leave out large chunks of revision on the basis of a forecast or guess at what might come up.

If you undertake the activities suggested above as you go through the course then you will build up brief or highlighted notes about the whole syllabus and these will be easier to revise quickly at the end. Remember we're trying to build confidence here through the use of a *well-planned approach* and trusting to luck doesn't support that notion.

③ ORGANISING NOTES AND OTHER COURSE MATERIALS

Part of ensuring that your final revision is as painless but effective as possible is having well organised course materials. You're likely to have a lot of stuff comprising:

- course text
- your own class notes
- summary key points
- notes on potential questions
- past exam papers
- marked coursework
- press and magazine articles.

You cannot afford to be confronted with a mass of disorganised papers just when you need to start your final preparations for the exam. Apart from being very daunting and unlikely to make you feel positive about the whole thing, your revision would take much longer than it needs to.

Organise your course materials from day one of the course.

Fortunately there's not a lot to say about how to do this but that doesn't make it any less important. Also, the way you keep materials is very much a matter of personal preference and knowing what will work for you.

- Loose-leaf files tend to be better than bound notebooks because you can add material later, thereby keeping everything relating to one topic together.

- Some students make very few notes but tend to use a highlight marker on printed course material. This can be done only if the materials are your own, not in school textbooks.

- Others make their own notes in class or from study texts.

You'll need to decide whether any notes you make are clear and tidy enough to be used for final revision. Rewriting can be time-consuming but does help consolidate your learning. Consolidation can also be achieved by reviewing your notes and highlighting or summarising key points for subsequent revision. Some students type all their written notes onto a PC each week. This is time consuming but they feel the investment is worthwhile.

Whichever method of record-keeping and summarising you choose, the aim should be to minimise the effort needed for final revision.

 PLANNING YOUR FINAL REVISION

We've talked about revision activities undertaken as you go through the course, including practising past questions, and we now need to think about your **final revision**. In Chapter 2 you saw that you need to plan some time for this. The time available will depend on your own circumstances but you must use it wisely. In most cases you'll be studying for more than one paper or subject so you must allocate the time between subjects in appropriate proportions.

You must produce a written plan.

The exams are important to you and you don't want to endure a re-sit. So set aside as much time as possible and do the revision in at least two stages:

1   Review your key notes, articles, model answers etc and condense the key notes into a final revision summary.

2   Review these summarised points.

During these stages you should also be doing at least a few practice questions. The format into which you condense your notes can be whatever you feel most comfortable with. The following have been used successfully:

- index cards

- single sheet summaries

- post-it notes stuck on a bedroom wall.

Do whatever suits you.

How early you start your *final* revision depends on your own circumstances. If you are given study leave by your school or your employer then so much the better. If not, or if this is minimal, you need to start the first stage earlier to ensure that you complete both stages in time for the exam.

Be sure to *plan some leisure time into your schedule.* You won't feel guilty taking planned breaks, especially if you've kept on schedule with your revision.

Any revision activities offered by your tutor should also be taken advantage of. Some students don't attend final lectures because '. . . it's only revision' but these sessions are likely to be extremely useful. They usually provide valuable insights into potential questions and how to answer them as well as identifying and explaining further the more complex bits of the course.

Plan a couple of hours at the end to re-read this book, or at least Chapters 1, 4 and 6.

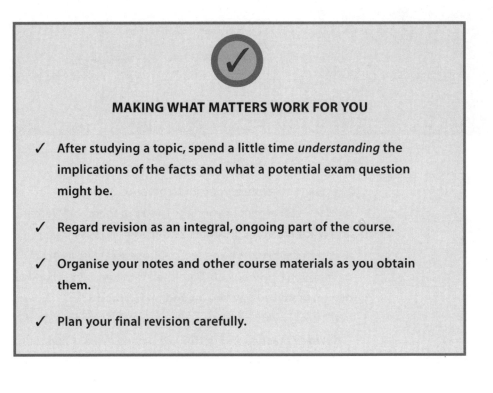

MAKING WHAT MATTERS WORK FOR YOU

✓ After studying a topic, spend a little time *understanding* the implications of the facts and what a potential exam question might be.

✓ Regard revision as an integral, ongoing part of the course.

✓ Organise your notes and other course materials as you obtain them.

✓ Plan your final revision carefully.

4 Writing Essays

Good essay technique means you can communicate clearly to the examiner who will then find it easy to allocate marks.

3 things that really matter

1 **KNOWING WHAT THE EXAMINER WANTS**

2 **PLANNING AND STRUCTURING YOUR ANSWER**

3 **PRESENTING ANSWERS CLEARLY AND MEANINGFULLY**

The ability to express yourself to others is a fairly fundamental aspect of your life. This applies to both verbal and written communications as well as to body language. In a written examination you will be judged at least as much on *how* you communicate with the examiner as on *what* you demonstrate you have learnt and understood.

It's not easy to learn effective writing skills, and much of it is down to practice and getting comments from others. But so far as **essays** are concerned there are some basic ground rules which are easy to understand and will help you get started. In this chapter we'll deal with these.

We've talked already about the need to practise exam questions. You now need to recognise that this is not just about being able to complete answers in the time available. It's also about gaining experience of *writing effectively* as a method of communication.

IS THIS YOU?

● *If I bombard the examiner with enough facts he'll see I've done the work and is bound to grant me a pass.* ● *Exams are not about demonstrating clever writing skills, they're about showing the examiner you've covered the course.* ● *There's not enough time in an exam to worry about how you present things, so I just concentrate on getting the facts down.* ● *I have very strong views on most things and I always try to get these across in an exam.*

① KNOWING WHAT THE EXAMINER WANTS

How often have you heard someone say '. . . she's worked really hard for her exams so she's bound to pass'? Sadly this isn't true unless effort is focused on the right things. In this context, 'the right things' are a combination of:

● **Learning** the course content.

● **Understanding** the key issues, arguments and viewpoints associated with the topic.

● **Thinking** about potential exam questions.

● **Practising** past and potential questions and getting feedback on your answers.

We'll see in Chapter 6 that how you approach the exam itself is also critical. For now, we'll look at some basic requirements for writing good exam answers.

The first thing you need to think about is *what exactly is the examiner looking for?* Remember:

● He wants you to pass.

● He likes to give marks.

But he's human, and when faced with a pile of exam scripts

to plough through in a tight time-scale he can do without you making it difficult for him. An unnecessarily long, barely legible, unstructured answer in which he has to search hard to find the things that he can give marks for is unlikely to do much for his health and temper. So throwing down all the facts and expecting him to sympathise with you because you've obviously done a lot of revision just *will not work*.

The examiner wants you to:

- Answer the question specifically as asked.

- Apply the course concepts and acknowledge source material.

- Show a clear understanding of the course content.

- Use logical and coherent arguments.

- Structure and present the essay in a way that's easy for him to follow.

- Write legibly.

- Use short sentences and paragraphs.

So the way in which you *structure and present your answer* is absolutely critical.

Developing the ability to write essays is every bit as important as learning the course content and ideas.

A well-structured and clearly presented essay conveys exactly the sort of impression that gets the examiner on your side straight away. In fact, if he can see that your plan and structure is logical and can easily pick out the key points, or even just the **key words**, it may well be that he won't even read the essay in detail. He'll just quickly award the marks for the key points and then move on. He will have been able to see easily and quickly that you know what you're doing so he can feel confident that he needn't waste time going though your answer with a fine-toothed comb.

Get the examiner on your side right from the start and make it easy for him to give you marks.

The first stage in all this is, of course, reading and understanding the question. We'll talk more about this in Chapter 6, but for now think about looking very closely at what the question asks. Below is a selection (not an exhaustive list) of the type of verbs used typically in essay questions and (my suggestions of) what they mean.

- **Account for**   Explain why something is so.

- **Analyse**   Explain the main points in detail.

- **Argue**   Make a case for and/or against a particular viewpoint and backed up with objective evidence.

- **Assess**   Using your knowledge of the course judge the degree to which something is so.

- **Compare**   Identify similar characteristics and differences between two or more things.

- **Contrast**   Point out differences between (and possibly, briefly acknowledge similarities).

- **Criticise**   Judge something showing its shortcomings backed with logical argument to support your criticism.

- **Describe**   Give a detailed account.

- **Discuss**   Examine the case for and against.

- **Explain**   Show clearly why something is so.
- **Identify**   Pick out key features.
- **Illustrate**   Explain something with examples.
- **Justify**   Show reasons for.
- **List**   Compile a list.
- **Prove**   Show, with evidence, why something is so.
- **Review**   Survey and make an assessment of something.
- **Summarise**   State the main points.
- **Trace**   Show the development of the history of something, explaining the various stages.
- **Verify**   Show why something is true.

When you look at and practise past papers, look out for key verbs and get into the habit of focusing your answers accordingly.

 PLANNING AND STRUCTURING YOUR ANSWER

You cannot write a good essay without **planning** it first. Having read the question carefully and identified the **key verb** or verbs, you need to think about how you will tackle your answer. You'll be starting to think of the main points and these will generate further thoughts which you'll be anxious to get down on paper.

Pause briefly and think about how you can capture these thoughts, ideas and facts in a way that ensures you will produce a clear, logical and well structured answer. By all means get your thoughts down on paper but *starting to write your answer immediately isn't the best way.* Jot your thoughts down in the form of a plan.

A plan will help you to:

- Collect your thoughts.

- Sort your ideas into a logical sequence.

- Structure your answer sensibly.

- View the answer as a whole and ensure it works towards a logical conclusion.

- Avoid repetition.

- Include all the key points.

Having thoughtfully constructed a plan you will be much more able to write fluently. If you don't do a plan then you will write things as they occur randomly to you and the result will be an uncoordinated mess.

An essay plan will save you time by giving a clear structure to follow. You are bound to produce a much better essay as a result.

- Make sure that the plan addresses exactly what is required. Refer to the key words in the question. If the question asks for 'Advantages and Disadvantages' then your plan should include these **headings**.

- Plan the **order** of the paragraphs in a way that develops the answer in a coherent fashion.

- Plan each **paragraph,** showing the main points.

- Your plan can take the form of **brief notes** or a **diagram**.

- Leave **spaces** to add things that occur as you clarify your thoughts.

- Refer to your plan regularly whilst writing your answer to make sure that you stay on track.

There will be three main parts to the structure:

- **The introduction**. Brief outline commenting on the topic and showing that you have understood the question. But don't indicate any conclusions at this stage. Include any assumptions or interpretations you have made regarding the question.

- **The main body**. Containing the key course concepts as they relate to the question. Most of the marks will be awarded for this section.

- **The conclusion**. Sum up and answer the question. It does not have to side with any particular argument if the facts are not overwhelming and can refer to other factors or further information that may be relevant.

The main body *must* be split into paragraphs and you'll probably find that the introduction and conclusion will require more than just one.

Consider carefully how your answer will lead from the initial question to the final conclusion. Think about how the arguments will develop logically and, therefore, what each paragraph will include.

Whilst sketching out your plan refer back regularly to the question and ensure that you are going to :

- *Answer the question*, and not try to write all you know about a topic.

- *Draw on relevant course material*. This is what examiners expect, what they can evaluate and what they will award marks for. Introducing material from outside the course can be useful to add meaning but the bulk of your answer must be directly related to the syllabus.

- *Show that you have understood* the course concepts and that you can express them in your own words.

- *Construct a clear logical argument.* There needs to be a coherent progression of ideas and arguments, a **thread** if you like, running through your answer.

- *Present a conclusion* that looks back over the main body and effectively answers the question. Remember, this doesn't mean that you have to take one side or the other in a particular argument unless specifically asked to do so (and even then you must acknowledge opposing views). In fact you need to be very careful about taking sides - you run the risk of appearing biased.

In particular, any political views must be avoided. Comments like 'the current government has made a complete mess of managing inflation' will almost certainly lose you marks. For one thing this would show that you're not being completely objective. And for another, there's always the risk that the examiner is a lifelong supporter of the current administration. The exam is not the place to air any political preferences.

I once studied with a very clever chap, an Oxford graduate, who repeatedly failed an economics paper in a professional examination. This surprised everyone and he was in serious danger of being unable to qualify in his chosen field. In conversation one day he said 'I have very strong political views and I always make sure I get these across in the exam'. It was pointed out to him that this was likely to be the reason for his repeated failures and he passed at the next attempt.

Where it's difficult to come to a clear view you can say that the arguments are inconclusive or that there are merits on either side dependent on circumstances. What you must be able to show is that you have *understood the key arguments on each side.* That is what will earn you the marks.

The examiner is looking for an objective analysis and reasoned arguments based on your understanding of the course content.

 PRESENTING ANSWERS CLEARLY AND MEANINGFULLY
You've gathered your thoughts and done an outline plan. You now need to craft a clear and easy to read answer. Your writing style should be **simple** and **direct:**

- Use **simple words**, eg 'start' not 'commencement'.

- Don't use several words where one will do, eg 'Now' not 'At this point in time'.

- Keep **sentences** short, ie 10–25 words maximum.

- Use **active verbs** not passive ones, eg 'The committee agreed that' not 'It was agreed by the committee'.

All of the above will make it easier for the examiner to read and understand. And that's what you want.

We've talked already about dividing the essay into **three main sections**. Within each section your answer must be split into paragraphs. Many students write one continuous piece of prose which is very difficult to read and to make sense of. The examiner will not appreciate this.

- Paragraphs should be short and cover *one* main idea. Don't be concerned about having too many paragraphs. Provided the content is relevant, the **division into paragraphs** makes it easier to read.

- The first sentence should **explain explicitly** the main

idea of that paragraph, eg 'Hitler underestimated the difficulties in achieving his plan to invade Britain'.

- The paragraph should then **elaborate** on the various reasons why and **conclude** with a brief evaluation of the **main theme**. View each paragraph as a mini-essay.

- Leave a couple of lines extra between paragraphs in case you need to go back and add something later.

As well as being short, each **sentence** should contain **one point**. These points should follow logically from one sentence to the next, developing the argument in your essay.

Punctuation and **grammar** are also important, but I'm only talking about being able to get the basics right. If you don't think you're as good as you ought to be in these areas you may find it useful to get hold of a brief guide. Most large bookshops stock these and they can be incredibly useful and take only a short time to read. As well as creating a bad impression and making your answer difficult to read, incorrect punctuation and grammar can actually change the sense of what you're trying to say.

The likely effects of bad **spelling** are a little more difficult to be sure about. You shouldn't actually lose marks for incorrect spelling but there is always the danger of creating a bad impression. The way to deal with it is to ensure that all other aspects of your essay style are up to scratch.

An examiner would find it very difficult to condemn a well structured, well argued and clearly presented essay if all that was wrong with it was poor spelling.

Finally, a word about **handwriting**. Some people have much clearer handwriting than others and there's nothing to be ashamed of if yours isn't the best (doctors seem to have coped for years!). But think of the examiner. If it's extremely difficult for her to read your script then she's unlikely to feel over-charitable about awarding marks. Handwriting also suffers as panic sets in – so don't let it!

All I can suggest if your writing is difficult to read is that you practise making it a little clearer. If you combine this with a really well laid out answer in terms of paragraph and sentence construction, then I'm sure you'll be OK. Examiners are used to dealing with poor handwriting because answers are written quickly, but you need to be aware of the difference between poor and illegible.

MAKING WHAT MATTERS WORK FOR YOU

✓ Make sure you can demonstrate a clear *understanding* of the key issues, arguments and viewpoints associated with each course topic.

✓ Take a little time to *plan* both the content and structure of your answer.

✓ Pay particular attention to the *layout* and *style* of your answer.

5 As the Exam Approaches

Stay positive and in control. Use your time wisely and don't be too hard on yourself.

4 things that really matter

1 **MAINTAINING CONFIDENCE AND CONTROL**

2 **REMINDING YOURSELF WHAT THE EXAM IS ABOUT**

3 **USING FINAL REVISION TIME EFFECTIVELY**

4 **LOOKING AFTER YOURSELF**

You've now disregarded the common myths about exams and taken control of the whole process. You've planned your study and revision time and gained a clear understanding of the syllabus as well as the likely *types* of question. The month or so leading up to the exam is a critical time because you must do the things which will ensure that you walk into the exam room feeling confident.

It doesn't have to be too painful. Of course you will have a lot of revision to cover but a marathon read-through of everything is not the way to succeed. You need to *plan your revision, vary the workload* a bit and *share thoughts* with some carefully chosen course colleagues. You must also plan your revision in such a way that you revise at a time of day that suits you best, and most importantly, in a way that gives you some time off even in the last few days.

IS THIS YOU?

The last month is the worst. The pressure builds up and I find it difficult to cope with all the work. • Final revision has to be about cramming during every spare hour that I have. • I've got more than one exam to do and I just don't know how to plan my revision. • During the last couple of weeks I get really miserable because I just can't do anything except revise. And if I try to give myself a break I feel really guilty.

① MAINTAINING CONFIDENCE AND CONTROL

You've seen how you can take control of the process and you've planned your approach like a well executed military campaign. But as you get closer to the exam those nagging doubts and long-held feelings about exams start to surface again. There's a simple answer to this – *don't let them!*

Each time a negative thought enters your head about the exam, replace it with a positive one.

You can find plenty of reasons to be positive in this book, so keep it to hand and refer to it if you start to get a little anxious. Remind yourself that:

- no one is trying to catch you out

- everyone wants you to pass (including the examiner!)

- and success is all down to your effort and technique.

Have another look at Chapter 1 and remind yourself of the grand conspiracy going on in your favour, not against you.

Remember that the techniques explained here account for *at least 50 per cent of your chances of success.* The other 50 per cent is down to the work you have to do in covering the course work and revision activities. That's the harder bit and takes up a fair amount of time over the academic year. Reading and understanding this book is the easy bit but is just as important. The really good thing is that you can read it in a couple of hours, so why not read it all again in the run-up to the exam? Seriously, as a minimum *you must read Chapter 6 just before each exam* – it contains absolutely essential and invaluable advice.

You can't afford to let nagging doubts get the better of you. This would endanger your otherwise excellent chances of success.

Stay in control of the situation, don't let the situation control you.

I've talked about working with other people and I'll be saying a little more about this below. But there can be a very negative, destructive effect also from taking too much notice of others. You can start to presume that they're cleverer than you are and that they've done much more work than you have. Then your confidence takes a knock and you start to become anxious again. Some of this is due to the loud braggarts we've all come across, but they're few and far between and are best avoided. Remember also that your reaction to others' posturing is your own responsibility and you can choose to ignore them. But mostly these fears are not a result of others' actions, *they're all in your own head.* Tell yourself:

- I am in control and I can cope.

- I've done everything possible to ensure that I will pass.

- Other people's actions are irrelevant to my success. I work in a way that suits me.

- I will plan my revision carefully and I can get it done in time.

- Unlike most candidates, I now have the techniques for success.

If you're one of these individuals who think that 'I always do badly in exams', you needn't think that any more. Exams are not a problem for those who have approached the course with the right attitude. Exams have become a problem through myth, irrationality and as something to blame by those who haven't worked and therefore, don't deserve to pass. In fact, by the time you enter the exam room the worst is over, all the hard work has been done and you now have two or three hours to show how well you can do.

Exams are easy! The challenging bit is completing the course and doing the revision.

 REMINDING YOURSELF WHAT THE EXAM IS ABOUT
Remember it's not a memory test. It aims to test your **understanding** of the course topics and ideas. So it's important in the last few weeks to bear this in mind and *plan your revision* including some time to:

- Review your notes of potential questions (see Chapter 3).

- Practise some essays under exam conditions.

- Look at as many past questions as you can and compile a brief essay plan for each to see how you would answer it.

- Think about essay technique and the things you learned in Chapter 4. In particular, remind yourself of the need to write concise, legible, well structured answers that will make it easy for the examiner to allocate marks.

● Make sure you understand the structure of the exam paper, ie how many questions you will be required to answer and how the marking scheme works.

You will need to demonstrate to the examiner in a clear and concise manner that you have understood and are able to apply the course concepts.

 USING FINAL REVISION TIME EFFECTIVELY

We talked about active revision in Chapter 4, so by the time the exam draws near you've already made some revision notes of the main points. You now need to read through all of your course material well in advance of the exam date. At this stage you may wish to edit your revision notes (or compile them if you haven't previously) to provide something that can be reviewed more quickly at final revision stage.

Some students even **summarise** their revision notes further to a level at which they can briefly review the main concepts in a few hours on the day before the exam. How far you go in this respect is really up to you. But what is important is that you don't expect to revise all of your notes and coursework in one marathon reading session very close to the exam.

This **multi-stage approach** doesn't just mean that you end up with a nice set of revision notes. There is actually another great advantage. Having had more than one review of your notes you will have consolidated your learning very effectively and this alone will help you to:

- Recall facts more easily.

- Get through your final revision more quickly.

Active Revision and summarising notes eases the final workload and helps your memory.

Your final revision needs to be carried out *as close as possible to the exam date.* The techniques referred to above will certainly help you to achieve this but you will need to compile carefully a **written final revision timetable** as follows:

- Determine the time available. Ideally you need some study leave from school, college or work. Those at work may wish to supplement this with some holiday entitlement (it's probably worth the investment in the longer term).

- Note any unavoidable commitments.

- Build some free time into your schedule for relaxation etc and don't feel guilty about it (see Looking After Yourself below).

- Divide the remaining time between the various subjects.

Continuing the theme of self-help groups (Chapter 4), some students find that spending a little time revising with others can be very productive. This involves all parties having prepared by reading the appropriate material and then discussing the key points and likely exam questions. The advantages are:

- It breaks the monotony and isolation of revising alone.

- Students can learn a great deal through hearing the views of others which often spark off further ideas.

- It provides valuable moral support at a time when there is a danger of anxiety rearing its head again.

- It helps maintain the process of **understanding** rather than simply revising facts.

Remember though the emphasis must be on *equal contributions* by all involved, so everyone must come to the sessions well prepared. Your time is very valuable at this stage so these meetings must be made to work well. An ideal number for such a group is you plus two or three others and you should meet regularly for, say, an hour or so.

Plan your revision carefully and maintain at least a little contact with some carefully selected course colleagues.

④ LOOKING AFTER YOURSELF

You cannot afford to neglect yourself in terms of mind, body and spirit. You're probably feeling a little anxious as the exam approaches and you have a lot to do. You may find that you neglect some of the important things in your life such as:

- Your social life.

- Relaxation and leisure time.

- Time with your family.

- Healthy eating and drinking. Many students tend to overdose on coffee and tea. Sipping water regularly is much better in terms of maintaining your energy levels.

- Exercise.

Of course your free time will be restricted but *you must have time for yourself* so plan some breaks into your schedule. If you have study leave, so that whole days are allocated to revision, then don't expect to work all day. Somewhere between five and seven hours solid revision per day is all most people can expect to do. And if you achieve this level of work then you can feel very pleased with yourself. A useful approach is to:

- Find the time of day that suits you best for studying. For me it's very early morning, some people work better late at night.

- Plan your revision time during these periods and, equally important, plan time off during the rest of the day.

For me, working first and rewarding myself with time off afterwards was a successful approach. Whilst on study leave, I worked from 7a.m. until around 3.30p.m. *with coffee, lunch and tea breaks* and had every evening free. I knew that I was incapable of absorbing information for more than five to seven hours so I didn't let myself feel guilty for having the rest of the time off. I have known this strategy work well for many people. It requires discipline but you can have planned breaks and view them as *a reward for hard work*.

If you don't have much time for final revision, eg if you are in employment and forced to revise in the evenings and at weekends, then it's not so easy. But the basic principle still applies. You must *plan breaks into the schedule*.

Pay careful attention also to your **diet** and **exercise**. Healthy eating and drinking, and short walks or even strenuous exercise, will help your mental state and you'll revise more effectively. During these last few weeks avoid late nights or excessive alcohol intake but maintain at least some sort of **social life** and form of relaxation.

Your aim must be to arrive at the exam in as good a physical and mental state as possible. So don't tire yourself out with work or wear yourself out with the wrong type of lifestyle.

All of this becomes even more critical in the last day or two before the exam.

- Don't burn the midnight oil the night before the exam. You should be skimming through revision notes only. I suggest that by 7p.m. at the latest you should close your books and tell yourself 'That's it, all the hard work is over, all I need to do now is think about my exam technique'. This is covered in Chapter 6 and at that stage is the only reading you should do.

- Check you have everything you need in terms of pens, pencils, rulers, calculators, spare batteries (or ideally, a spare calculator) etc for the following day. It's a good idea to make up a written checklist well in advance.

- Recheck the time of the exam. I have known instances where students turned up in the afternoon for an exam held in the morning!

- Have a relaxing evening and go to bed early enough to get a good night's sleep.

- Don't attempt to do any revision on the morning of the exam. It's too late, and tends to create feelings of panic.

- On the morning of the exam, have breakfast and concentrate only on getting to the venue on time and unflustered. If you're not familiar with the location then check out train and bus times in advance. If you're driving make sure you know whether you'll have any traffic jams to deal with and where you can park. Make sure you have contingency plans to cover delays or cancellations of public transport, unforeseen traffic problems etc.

- Arrive in the vicinity of the exam early and find somewhere quiet to sit and breathe deeply to calm yourself.

- Avoid contact and conversation with other students. Alternatively, strike a deal with your colleagues that, even if you meet on the morning of the exam, you will not discuss it. It won't help any of you and some of you will start to panic because you will think (probably wrongly) that others are better prepared.

- Allow yourself to feel a little nervous, it'll get the adrenaline flowing and bring out the best in you.

Arrive at the exam calm, collected, refreshed and cautiously optimistic.

MAKING WHAT MATTERS WORK FOR YOU

✓ Don't allow anxiety to take over now, get rid of negative thoughts and stay in control.

✓ Remember that the exam will test your understanding and application of the course.

✓ Plan your final revision carefully and stick to your plan.

✓ Pay particular attention to your physical and mental health.

6 The Exam Itself

*Failure through poor exam technique is very
common, even for hard working, clever students.
But the good news is that the types of mistake are
also very common and are easily avoided.*

Techniques for dealing with the exam itself are as important as revising thoroughly.

A tutor once remarked that with proper technique you can achieve a pass in any exam without even knowing anything about the subject! An exaggeration perhaps, but the point is well made.

Ironically, the effort needed to master these techniques is minimal but the results can be quite amazing. The techniques are easy to use and can be referred to quickly as a last minute reminder.

Students who have covered the course and revised well have already done the hard bit. Using the techniques outlined in this chapter they can virtually guarantee success. Those who have not worked so hard may well find also that the use of these techniques will partly compensate for a lack of knowledge giving a pleasant surprise when the results are received.

IS THIS YOU?

● *I get really keyed up just before the exam and, all of a sudden, I think I won't be able to remember anything I've revised.* ● *I like to read the exam paper quickly and get stuck into the first question as soon as I've got a rough idea what's required. I get really worried seeing other people well underway when I've hardly started.* ● *I always run out of time so I think a good approach is to answer fewer questions than required but do them really well.* ● *I hate finding out after the exam that I misunderstood a question. But I usually console myself that I've written enough to show the examiner that I know all about the subject really.*

① STAYING COOL, CONFIDENT, CALM AND RELAXED

By now you should be feeling pretty positive. In Chapter 1 you saw how to get a perspective on exams. Chapter 2 showed you how to take control of the whole process and in the last chapter you saw that the worst is over because all the hard work has been done. But it's only natural to feel a little apprehensive, and that's fine as long as this is supported by an underlying feeling of quiet confidence.

A little nervous tension can bring out the best in you during the exam.

- If panic starts to set in go somewhere quiet and take a few deep breaths.

- Smile to yourself – it will help.

- Don't allow any negative thoughts to take hold. Replace them immediately with positive ones.

- Don't do any last-minute revision - other than reading this chapter.

② READING THE EXAM PAPER AND SELECTING QUESTIONS

Stay calm, keep up the slow, deep breathing or anything else that works for you and spend about five minutes reading the instructions and all the questions. The people in the room who begin writing within about a minute of getting the paper are well on the way to failure. But you should be ignoring everyone else anyway. Their writing speed and requests for extra paper are totally irrelevant to your chances of success.

Don't hunt frantically for the first topic that looks vaguely familiar and start your first answer.

- Read the instructions at the top so you know how many questions you have to answer.

- Then read the questions carefully to understand exactly what each one asks.

- Recheck the instructions for how many you need to select.

- Begin the selection process.

Remember, it's extremely unlikely that you will be asked to 'Write all you know about . . .' So don't select a question solely on the basis of the subject content. You saw in Chapter 4 how to look for *exactly* what you are required to do. Look for words like:

- analyse

- assess

- compare

- describe

- explain

- discuss

- illustrate

- list

. . . and make sure you can, for the subject involved.

You will be judged critically on whether you have done what you were asked to do.

Once you've selected your questions, answer your best one first. This will boost your confidence. **Multiple choice questions** require a similar approach. In particular:

- Read the instructions carefully and underline key words in the questions as you get to them.

- Check the **sense** of the question. Look out for negatives and double negatives.

- Look out for answers that are almost identical.

- Don't underestimate multiple choice exams, they are every bit as testing as written ones and they aim to test your understanding very carefully.

- Don't even think about doing minimal work and guessing randomly. The odds are not in your favour.

- Some students adopt a special approach which you might like to consider. They mentally answer the question without looking at any of the choices listed. They then look for the answer that corresponds to their own, not having been led by confusing wording.

③ MANAGING YOUR TIME

The examination paper is put together very carefully and sufficient time is allowed to complete it.

- The intention is that you should complete it.

- Furthermore you are *instructed* to answer a specific number of questions.

The strategy of *answering fewer questions* but doing them 'really well' is seriously flawed. Not only have you have ignored the carefully considered instructions, but you are also seriously reducing your chances of success. Assuming 20 marks per question, a student who answers four questions rather than five immediately limits the maximum marks obtainable to 80 per cent. If the pass mark is 50 per cent then he must achieve an average of 62.5% over four questions. This is much more difficult to achieve than 50 per cent per question. It's as simple as that.

The way to avoid the problem is also very simple:

- Allocate your time proportionately.

- Spend no more than the allotted time on each question.

For example, if the examination is three hours long and the required number of questions give 100 marks, then you have 180 minutes to gain a maximum of 100 marks. This allows 1.8 minutes per mark, so for a 20-mark question you should allow 20 times 1.8 minutes giving 36 minutes. You may decide to allow yourself 30 minutes with six minutes' reading time at the end. Similarly, for a ten-mark question in a three-hour paper you should allow a total of 18 minutes. In a two-hour paper this would be 12 minutes (1.2 minutes per mark).

You must then *monitor your time carefully* throughout

each question and aim to finish it on time. As you reach the final few minutes, wind up your essay.

After spending the allotted time on a question, leave it and move on immediately to the next - whatever stage you have reached in your answer.

Many students find great difficulty in moving on from a question before they have finished, but it is vital that you do. Apart from the need to maximise your potential marks, the points likely to be gained in the final few minutes are likely to be considerably less than those gained in the opening few minutes of the next question. So you may spend an extra ten minutes (that you don't have) in chasing one or two marks as opposed to gaining seven or eight on the next question.

● Try to wrap up any essays as you approach the end time or leave some space on your answer sheet to return to if you find time later.

Provided you have revised sufficiently there is absolutely no excuse for answering less than the required number of questions.

The rules are the same for multiple choice questions. Allocate your time proportionately and move on after the allotted time. The time available for each question will of course be small but you must avoid the tendency to get bogged down on any one question. If you're struggling with a question don't guess at the answer. Move on and come back to it at the end. If you're still unsure, then just give it your best shot.

 READING THE QUESTION
You've already read the question at selection stage but

before beginning your answer you must re-read it and:

- underline or highlight key words

- identify any separate components.

Consider the question: 'Outline the events leading to the outbreak of the Second World War. Comment on the assertion that Britain could have avoided declaring war on Germany'. The words 'outline', 'second' and 'comment' are critical and should be highlighted. Also note that there are two distinct parts to the question and the marking scheme will reflect this. The answer must be divided into two parts, not amalgamated into a single narrative. *This is the start of your essay planning process.*

For questions split into the format (a), (b), (c) it is easier to identify the component parts but these should still be scrutinised for key words. Then *read the question again before you begin your answer.* You should have read it carefully at least three times before you start.

Examiners' reports repeatedly comment that students have not read the questions properly. Tension, panic and the desire to get stuck in are often the cause but you cannot afford to risk such a fundamental mistake. Having spent months on a course of study and revision it's little short of tragic to fail for the sake of a few minutes composing yourself and going through the simple steps outlined above. Think about it.

⑤ ANSWERING THE QUESTION

Having read the question and understood exactly what's required you are now well placed to write a clear and well focused answer.

Remember, your aim is to make the answer easy for the examiner to read and understand, and therefore, easy to award marks in accordance with the pre-determined scheme.

A word of warning though. For essay-type answers students regularly lose that clear focus and drift off into irrelevancies. So how do you avoid this? It's easy - remember from Chapter 4:

- You must construct a brief essay plan.

This will take up more valuable time, but it will save you at least as much time by giving you a clear structure to follow. You are bound to construct a better essay as a result.

- This will impress the examiner and help clarify your approach.

- Give your plan a heading (e.g. 'Question 3 plan') and hand it in with your answer.

- Make sure that the plan addresses exactly what is required. Refer to the key words in the question. If the question asks for 'advantages and disadvantages' then your plan should include these headings.

- Plan each paragraph showing the main points to be covered.

- Your plan can take the form of brief notes or a diagram (mind map).

- Leave spaces to add things that occur as you clarify your thoughts.

- Refer to it regularly whilst writing your answer so that you stay on track.

Remember that you must maintain a clear focus on what has been asked for. Don't lapse into 'write all you know about . . .' mode. This will not impress the examiner. It will simply make it more difficult for him to allocate marks. *And don't waste time writing out the question at the beginning of your answer.*

⑥ WHAT TO DO AFTER THE EXAM

When the invigilator tells you that the time is up he might as well add, 'You are now free to leave and undermine each other's confidence'. Because this is exactly what happens; candidates leave the room and immediately begin comparing how they approached certain questions, what they included, what they assumed was asked for etc. Those who found it difficult will be unnerved even more by others who say they found it straightforward or easy. This is all completely pointless. There is nothing to be gained from worrying about something over which you have no control.

- If your exams are over simply forget about them and await the result.

- If you have other papers to take, concentrate on those. Getting depressed about the previous one will serve only to affect your chances adversely.

I was absolutely convinced I'd failed an examination once. I had found it difficult whilst several of my colleagues commented that they'd found it easy. I began studying for a retake and even bought additional textbooks. I didn't wait at home for the postman on the day that the results were due. I had in fact passed.

Even if you think you've done badly, you may well get a pleasant surprise, especially if you've followed the advice given in this chapter.

Agree with your colleagues in advance that you will not enter into post-mortems. Otherwise, simply leave the building alone after the exam . . . and forget about it!

MAKING WHAT MATTERS WORK FOR YOU

✓ Allow yourself a little nervous tension but, equally, ensure an underlying feeling of quiet confidence.

✓ Read the instructions and questions carefully. Make sure you know how many questions you need to do. Highlight key words to determine exactly what each question is asking for.

✓ Allocate your time to ensure that you will complete the examination. Move on as soon as the allotted time is up for each question.

✓ Read each question carefully before answering, highlight key words and identify all component parts.

✓ Plan your answer and refer to the plan regularly as you write.

✓ Avoid post-mortems.